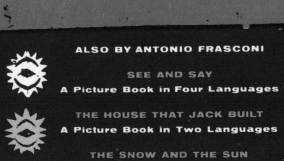

A Picture Book in Four Languages

SEE AGAIN
SAY AGAIN

guarda di nuovo
parla di nuovo

regarde de nouveau
parle de nouveau

mira de nuevo
habla de nuevo

WOODCUTS BY ANTONIO FRASCONI

harcourt, brace & world, inc., new york

As a father, I want my children to know and to understand that today many languages are spoken in our own back yard and to realize that a foreign language is not alien any more. A child should be aware that there are many ways to name the same object, that this world is composed of many peoples and many lands.

Throughout the book you will find the words for each object in English, Italian, French, and Spanish, together with a guide to the pronunciation. The following color key has been used: black for English words; blue for Italian words; red for French words; green for Spanish words. There is also a page of everyday expressions.

A. F.

spring
spring

primavera
pree-mah-veh'-rah

printemps
pran-tawng

primavera
pree-mah-veh'-rah

woods
wudz

village
vill'-edj

bosco
boh'-skoh

villaggio
veel-lah'-djoh

bois
bwah

village
vee-lahzh

bosque
bohs'-keh

aldea
ahl-deh'-ah

sunset

sun'-set

tramonto

trah-mon'-toh

coucher de soleil

koo'-shay duh soh-lehya

puesta del sol

pwehs'-tah dell sahl

mountain

moun'-ten

montagna

mohn-tah'-n'yah

montagne

mohn-tahn

montaña

mohn-tah'-n'yah

summer
sum'-er

estate
ehs-tah'-teh

été
a-tay

verano
veh-rah'-noh

traffic
traff'-ick

traffico
trahf'-fee-koh

trafic
trah-feek'

trafico
trah'-fee-koh

beach
beech

spiaggia
sp'yah'-djah

plage
plahzh

playa
plah'-yah

sand
sand

sabbia
sahb'-b'yah

sable
sahbl

arena
ah-reh'-nah

autumn
aw'-tum

autunno
ow-toon'-noh

automne
oh-tun

otoño
oh-toh'-n'yoh

field
feel'd

campo
kahm'-poh

champ
shawng

campo
kahm'-poh

factory
fack'-tree

fabbrica
fah'-bree-kah

fabrique
fahb-reek'

fabrica
fah'-bree-kah

moon

moon

luna

loo'-nah

lune

lewn

luna

loo'-nah

harvest

hahrv'-ist

raccolto

rahk-koll'-toh

moisson

mwah-sohn

cosecha

koh-seh'-chah

winter
wint'r

inverno
een-vehr'-noh

hiver
ee-vair'

invierno
een-v'yehr'-noh

skiing
skee'-ing

sci
shee

ski
skee

esquiismo
es-kee-ees'-mo

sledding
sled'-ding

lo slittare
loh zleet-tah'-reh

luge
lewzh

ir en trine
eer en tree-neh'-yo

snow   **neve**   **neige**   **nieve**

snoh   *neh'-veh*   *nehzh*   *n'yeh'-veh*

skating   **pattinaggio**   **patinage**   **patinaje**

ayt'-ing   *paht-tee-nah'-djoh*   *pah-teen-azh*   *pah-tee-nah'-heh*

railroad crossing
rayl'-rohd kraw'-sing

passaggio a livello
pahs-sah'-djoh ah lee-vehl'-loh

passage à niveau
pah-sahzh ah nee-voh

cruce de trenes
kroo'-seh deh treh'-nehs

stop
stop

stop
stop

arrêtez
ah-reh'-teh

pare
pah'-reh

bus stop
buhss stop

fermata dell'autobu
fehr-mah'-tah dell'ow'-toh-boos

arrêt de l'autobus
ah-reh duh low-toh-bewss

parada de autobus
pah-ra'-dah deh ah-o-toh-boos'

sign
sigh'n

insegna
een-sehn'-yah

enseigne
aw-seh-nyeh

letrero
leh-treh'-roh

danger
dayn'-jer

pericolo
peh-ree'-koh-loh

danger
dawn-zhay

peligro
peh-lee'-groh

no parking
noh par'-king

vietato il parcheggio
v'yeh-tah'-toh eel pahr-keh'-djoh

stationnement interdit
stah-s'yohn-mawng an-tehr-dee

se prohibe estacionar
seh proh-ee'-beh ehs-tah-s'yoh-nahr'

apartment
apart'-munt

appartamento
ahp-pahr-tah-mehn'-toh

appartement
ah-pahr-tuh-mawng

apartamiento
ah-pahr-tah-m'yehn'-toh

window
wind'-oh

finestra
fee-nehs'-trah

fenêtre
fuh-netr

ventana
vehn-tah'-nah

bedroom
bed'-room

stanza da letto
stahn'-tsah dah leht-toh

chambre à coucher
shawm' br ah koo'-shay

dormitorio
dohr-mee-toh'-r'yoh

iving room
'-ing room

salotto
ah-lot'-toh

salon
ah-lohn

sala
ah'-lah

dining room
dye'-ning room

sala da pranzo
sah'-lah dah prahn'-dsoh

salle à manger
sahl ah mawn-zhay

comedor
koh-meh-dohr'

kitchen
kih'-chen

cucina
koo-chee'-nah

cuisine
kwee-zeen

cocina
koh-see'-nah

flowers
flau'-erz

fleurs
fluhr

fiori
f'yoh-ree

flores
floh'-rehs

keys
keez

chiavi
k'yah-vee

clefs
klay

llaves
lyah'-vehs

ink
ink

inchiostro
een-k'yohs'-troh

encre
awnkr

tinta
teen'-tah

matches
ma'-chz

fiammiferi
f'yahm-mee'-feh-ree

allumettes
ah-lew-met

fósforos
fohs'-foh-rohs

pen
pen

penna
pehn'-nah

plume
plewm

pluma
ploo'-mah

city
sih'-tee

città
cheet-tah'

ville
veel

ciudad
s'yoo-dahd

building
bill'-ding

edificio
eh-dee-fee'-choh

bâtiment
bah-tee-mawng

edificio
eh-dee-fee'-syoh

people
pee'-pl

gente
jehn'-teh

gens
zhawng

gente
hehn'-teh

sidewalk
sigh'd'-wawk

marciapiede
mahr-cha-p'yeh'-deh

trottoir
troh-twahr

acera
ah-seh'-rah

street
street

via
vee'-ah

rue
rew

calle
kah'-l'yeh

seal
seel

foca
foh'-kah

phoque
faw-k

foca
foh'-kah

monkey
munk'-ee

scimmia
sheem'-m'yah

singe
sanzh

mono
moh'-noh

tiger
ty'-gur

tigre
tee'-greh

tigre
teegr

tigre
tee'-greh

zoo
zoo

giardino zoologico
jahr-dee'-noh dzoh-oh-loh'-jee-koh

zoo
zoh

jardín zoológico
hahr-deen' zoh-oh-loh'-hee-koh

bear
bair

orso
or'-soh

ours
oorss

oso
oh'-soh

fruit
froot

frutta
froot'-tah

fruit
frwee

fruta
froo'-tah

apples
ap'-lz

mele
meh'-leh

pommes
pum

manzanas
mahn-tsah-nahz

pears
pairz

pere
peh'-reh

poires
pwahr

peras
peh'-rahss

plums
plumz

susine
soo-see'-neh

prunes
prewn

ciruelas
see-rweh-lahss

oranges	**arance**	**lemons**	**limoni**
'-ran-juz	*ah-rahn'-cheh*	*lem'-unz*	*lee-moh'-nee*
oranges	**naranjas**	**citrons**	**limones**
-rawnzh	*nah-rahn'-hahss*	*see-trohn*	*lee-moh'-nehs*

vegetables
vedj'-tuh-buhlz

legumi
leh-goo'-mee

légumes
lay-gewm

legumbres
leh-goom'-brehs

lettuce
let'-uss

lattuga
laht-too'-gah

laitue
lay-tew

lechuga
leh-choo'-gah

onion
un'-yun

cipolla
chee-pohl'-lah

oignon
oh-n'yohng

cebolla
seh-boh'-l'yah

carrot
kaer'-ut

carota
kah-roh'-tah

carotte
kah-roht

zanahoria
tzah-nah-oh'-r'yah

radish
rad'-ish

rafano
rah'-fah-noh

radis
rah-dee

rábano
rah'-bah-no

string beans
string beenz

fagiolini
fah-joh-lee'-nee

haricots verts
aree-ko vair

habichuelas verdes
ah-bee-chweh'-lahs vehr'-dehs

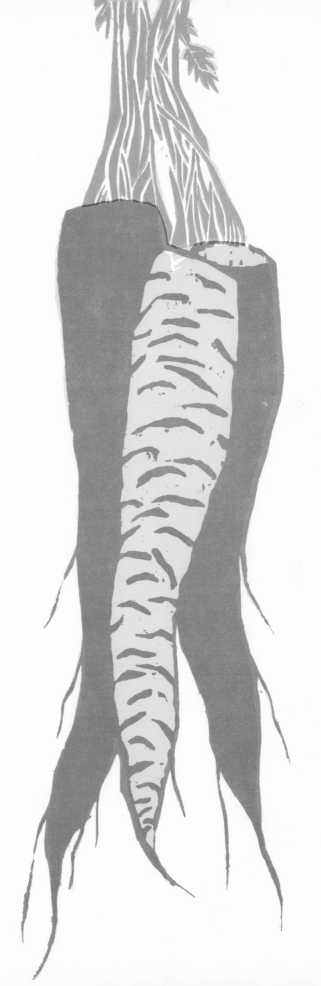

food
food

cibo
chee'-boh

nourriture
noo-ree-tewr

comida
koh-mee'-dah

meat
meet

carne
kahr'-neh

viande
v'yawnd

carne
kahr'-neh

butter
butt'-r

burro
boor'-roh

beurre
burr

mantequilla
mahn-teh-kee'-l'yah

cheese
cheez

formaggio
fohr-mah'-djoh

fromage
froh-mahzh'

queso
keh'-soh

milk
mill'k

latte
laht'-teh

lait
lay

leche
leh-cheh

bread
bred

pane
pah'-neh

pain
pa-n

pan
pahn

family
fam'-lee

famiglia
fah-mee'-l'yah

famille
fah-mee-yeh

familia
fah-mee'-l'yah

father
fah'-th'r

padre
pah'-dreh

père
pair

padre
pah'-dreh

brother
bruth'-r

fratello
frah-tehl'-loh

frère
frair

hermano
ehr-mah'-noh

mother
muth'-r

madre
mah'-dreh

mère
mair

madre
mah'-dreh

sister
sist'-r

sorella
soh-rehl'-lah

soeur
suhr

hermana
ehr-mah'-nah

grandmother
gran'-muth-r

nonna
nohn-nah

grand-mère
grawn-mair

abuela
ah-bweh'-lah

Excuse me.	Scusi.	Pardon.	Dispénseme.
ex-skewz mee	skoo'-zee	pahr-dohn	dees-pehn'-seh

Hello	Pronto	Allo	Hola
hel-lo	prohn'-toh	al-loh	oh'-lah

How much is it?	Quant'è?	Combien est-ce?	¿Cuánto es?
how mutch iz it	kwahnt'eh	kohn-bee-yahn ess	kwahn'-toh ehs

It is cold.	Fa freddo.	Il fait froid.	Hace frío.
it iz kold	fah fred'-doh	eel fay frwah	ah-seh free'-o

It is hot.	Fa caldo.	Il fait chaud.	Hace calor.
it iz haht	fah kahl'-doh	eel fay show	ah-seh kah-lor

It is raining.	Piove.	Il pleut.	Está lloviend
it iz rayn-ing	p'yoh'-veh	eel pluh	ehs-tah' lyoh-vee-yeh.

Thank you.	Grazie.	Merci.	Gracias.
thank yew	grah'-ts'yeh	mair-see	grah'-see'yahs

I am well.	Sto bene.	Je vais bien.	Estoy bien.
eye am wel	stoh beh'-neh	zhuh vay bee-yahn	ehs-toy' b'yehn

Please	Per piacere	S'il vous plaît	Por favor
pleez	pehr p'yah-cheh'-reh	seel voo pleh	pohr fah-vohr'

I am late.	Sono in ritardo.	Je suis en retard.	Estoy tarde.
eye am layt	soh'-noh een ree-tahr'-doh	zhuh swee zohn ruh-tarr	ehs-toy' tar-deh

I am early.	Sono in anticipo.	Je suis en avance.	Estoy tempra
eye am err'-lee	soh'-noh een ahn-tee'-chee-poh	zhuh swee zohn a-vahnss	ehs-toy' tehm-prah'-nc

I am hungry.	Ho fame.	J'ai faim.	Tengo hambr
eye am hung-gree	hoh fah'-meh	zhay fah-n	tehn'-goh om'-b

Yes	Sì	Oui	Sí
yess	see	wee	see

No	No	Non	No
noh	noh	nohn	noh